THE SPIRITUAL MAXIMS
OF
ST. FRANCIS DE SALES

✠

The
SPIRITUAL MAXIMS
of
ST. FRANCIS DE SALES

⊕

Edited and Introduced by
C. F. Kelley

Angelico Press

For information, address:
Angelico Press, Ltd.
4709 Briar Knoll Dr.
Kettering, OH 45429
www.angelicopress.com

ISBN: 978-1-887593-21-2
ISBN: 978-1-62138-615-5

NIHIL OBSTAT: John M. A. Fearns, S.T.D.
CENSOR LIBRORUM
IMPRIMATUR: Francis Cardinal Spellman
Archbishop of New York
July 24, 1953

Cover Design: Michael Schrauzer
Cover Image: mosaic, Chapel of Bl. Pius IX,
Basilica of San Lorenzo Fuori le Mura, Rome

CONTENTS

PART III

Introduction

The beginning of the seventeenth century found France, in fact all of Europe, unnerved by the Wars of the League; a great majority of the faithful were driven to despair by two spiritual evils. There had been so much suffering that many men and women readily believed that God took no interest in human affairs. How obvious the setting was for the cold philosophy of Montaigne! Others wandered into a spiritual wasteland with the conviction that the life of devotion was impossible for those whose work brought them into contact with the world of human commerce. For them there was only one solution—the penitent, cloistered, monastic life.

It was in this dry atmosphere that the fresh and warm teachings of St. Francis de Sales found a receptive and grateful audience. In many ways he was the anti-type of Calvin of the preceding century. He was far less constrained, more rounded, more alive. Even in picturing him we do not envisage him wearing a stiff, conventional collar to keep the head straight, permitting no grace of movement. He was led to God not by fear, but by love. Nor did he plunge into the distant past to find God. For St. Francis, God is *Emmanuel—God with us*—always present with us in His Universal Church. Moreover, if this saint answers the cold theory which ends in turning the back on God through fear of Him, he also answers that other reactionary trend which culminates in the presumption of exaggerated quietism. Never does he seek to destroy the will; he asks for an utter abandonment of the will to God, and such abandonment requires a most subtle act of the will.

Seeds of devotion were sown by St. Francis in a hundred different ways. With one person it would be no more than a brief counsel, but one never to be forgotten. With another it would be a verbal *apéritif* that marked the starting point for a more meaningful way of life. He took souls just where he found them in the midst of their ordinary occupations. With the help of ever-present grace, which transforms without changing, he elevated nature without altering it. Whatever could be turned to the service of God he permitted to bud and blossom, pruning, guiding and correcting when obviously necessary. In other words, he brought Christianity into every aspect of life by making the intention of pleasing God the center of man's actions. Indeed, it would be a short-sighted spirituality which did not bless the monastic life, and no one blessed it more than St. Francis de Sales. But he also taught people to believe that there was nothing to prevent them from seeing the beauty of God in every true vocation. Little by little the obstacles in the way of devotion became smaller for the layman as well as for the religious.

Read St. Francis and you feel that human nature is known, supported and uplifted; the affectionate side of man's nature, his passions and psychological longings are understood in terms of their roots. Here is a knowledge acquired by a priest who directed souls, by a bishop who truly shepherded his flock; here is a deep understanding which sprang from a holy man's affection for those whom he longed to make whole. Nothing is more piercing than affection. If we love we will know. And this helps to explain why the Saint placed so much emphasis on friendship as a vital support to man's true calling. It explains why he regarded the obedience we render to our neighbor, to our employer, to our doctor, as an important little virtue. It also explains why he believed the intellect must always be brought into play, for the will must be sharpened by clarity.

St. Francis does not address us *en masse*; he speaks to us as so many persons. We recognize ourselves in what is said because he speaks about things of which each of us has had experience. Somehow devotion is made more interesting than the affairs of the world. He does not start us off with anything very exciting, such as ecstasies or the experiential union with God about which most mystics speak. He begins with the little practical virtues of simplicity, humility, gentleness, fidelity. . . . Is not this just where a beginning should be made? "Opportunities," he writes to a friend, "seldom present themselves for the practice of great and heroic virtues, but each day presents us with a thousand occasions for practicing little virtues with a heroic spirit." If St. Francis does not always convince our intellects, he does touch our hearts and plant in them a wish to believe and love. And when a man wishes something to be true, he comes very close to finding it true.

He teaches love, and only love; a person who truly loves will sooner or later be loved in return. But love must be tranquil; eagerness even about doing good is suspect. "Even our faults," he says, "should be tranquilly despised." This is the kind of maxim the Jansenists as well as many of our present-day puritans and penitents fail to grasp. Should we act like the lion that was annoyed by the fly, or should we cultivate that patience which tries to see our faults and learn the lesson of humility which they are meant to teach? Here is a plumb bob that must be cast upward, not downward; for unless our hope is established in God's loving-kindness it is false hope. It is not on our own goodness that we must rely, but on God because He is Goodness itself.

Is this easy devotion? Some accuse St. Francis of leading people to heaven in a luxury liner. But would they say this if they really knew anything about spiritual matters? Does he ever encourage one to risk the shattering of the fortress of grace in the storm of worldly life? It is one thing to be an *honnête homme* in the world; it is quite another to perform every action for the love of God. But the St. Peter in us will not have it so; he always wants to do more. And if St. Francis tries to calm down that side of our nature, it is because he never forgets what happened to St. Peter. If he distrusts the zeal we manifest today, it is because he knows that it may too easily turn into aridity tomorrow, and lead us into that discouragement which is a total absence of love.

Most people, however, when they meet the wise and charming St. Francis in his writings, are unwilling to let him go. But much as one might like to carry his *Treatise on the Love of God* or a volume of his *Letters* to and from one's daily duties, these books are much too large and bulky for the average pocket. Hence this little collection of maxims and sayings gathered from those many pages of spiritual counseling. They are words of advice which every friend of St. Francis has always been fond of repeating—words which serve as props of encouragement, points for meditation, counsels, exhortations, reminders.

With this in mind, I have arranged these maxims in what I believe are convenient sections. However, the person who chooses to carry them about with him will soon discover that they can be properly digested only by taking them slowly and one at a time. He will also discover that he will want to add the books from which these maxims are gathered to his devotional shelf, for St. Francis speaks as much to our twentieth-century conditions as he did to the conditions of his own spiritual family.

The following books, then, are to be recommended: *Introduction to the Devout Life*, translated by John K. Ryan (New York: Harper, 1950). *Treatise on the Love of God, Letters to Persons in the World, Letters to Persons in Religion, Spiritual Conferences*, all translated and edited by Dom. B.

Mackey, O.S.B. (London: Burns, Oates and Washbourne, 1908). *St. Francis de Sales in His Letters* (London: Sands, 1933). *The Depositions of St. Jeanne de Chantal in the Cause of the Canonisation of St. Francis de Sales*, translated by Dom. Mackey, O.S.B. (London: Burns, Oates and Washbourne, 1908). *The Spirit of St. Francis de Sales*, by Jean Pierre Camus (New York: Harper, 1952).

C. F. KELLEY

June 15, 1953

KEY TO REFERENCES

I   *Introduction to the Devout Life*

T   *Treatise on the Love of God*

LW   *Letters to Persons in the World*

LR   *Letters to Persons in Religion*

C   *Spiritual Conferences*

S   *The Spirit of St. Francis de Sales*

D   *The Depositions of St. Jeanne de Chantal in the Cause of the Canonisation of St. Francis de Sales*

T—book /II—book /7—chapter or section

PART I

I

To Love or to Die

Between death and love there is no alternative. (LR VI 24)

Love and death are so mingled in the Passion of our Lord that we cannot have the one in our heart without the other. (T XII 13)

Love Alone

All is love's, and in love, for love, in holy Church. (T pref.)

Hatred separates us, and love brings us into one. (T I 9)

To live according to the spirit is to love according to the spirit; to live according to the flesh is to love according to the flesh; for love is the life of the soul as the soul is the life of the body. (LR III 47)

Love is the movement, effusion and advancement of the heart toward the good. (T I 7)

The affinity which causes love does not always consist in resemblance, but in the mutual relation between the lover and the thing loved. (T I 8)

Union in distinction makes order; order produces agreement; and proportion and agreement, in complete and finished things, make beauty. (T I 1)

The union to which love aspires is spiritual. (T I 10)

Love not finding us equal, equalizes us, not finding us united, unites us. (T III 13)

The end of love is no other thing than the union of the lover and the thing loved. (T I 9)

We cannot help conforming ourselves to what we love. (T VIII 1)

All is subject to heavenly love, who will either be king or nothing. (T I 6)

To love truly and to cease loving are two incompatible things. (LW VII 20)

Chaste and holy fear is a reverence, a love and respect, free from all that is servile or mercenary. (S I 16)

Love desires secrecy. (T VI 1)

You must grow in love by means of the root, rather than the branches. (s II 7)

Love is like fire, which is of clearer and fairer flame as its matter is more delicate. (T I 10)

Love is bittersweet, and while we live in this world it never has a sweetness perfectly sweet, because it is not perfect, nor ever purely satisfied. (T VI 13)

Love either takes away the hardship of labor, or makes it dear to us while we feel it. (T IX 2)

The Holy Ghost teaches that the lips of the Spouse, that is the Church, resemble *scarlet* and *the dropping honeycomb*, to let everyone know that all the doctrine which she announces consists *in sacred love*. (T pref.)

Love is the abridgment of all theology. (T VIII 1)

During this mortal life we must choose eternal love or eternal death, there is no middle choice. (T XII 13)

Man

Man is an epitome of the world; he is a little world in himself, in which all that is to be found in the great world of the universe is found. (C III)

Man is the perfection of the universe, the spirit is the perfection of man, love that of the spirit, and charity that of love. (T X 1)

You will never see God without goodness, nor yourself without misery. (LR I 2)

God is our God and man's heart is His home. (LR II 19)

God is in you as the heart of your heart and the spirit of your spirit. (IN II 2)

Man has a natural inclination to love God above all things. (T I 16)

Nothing so much presses man's heart as love. (T VII 8)

God has imprinted on all created things His traces, trail or footsteps. (T III 9)

God is God of the human heart. (T I 15)

What was I when I was not? What was I, who now being something am yet but a simple and poor worm of the earth? (T XII 12)

All that is good *in* us, is not *of* us. (S XIX 3)

What can we do of ourselves but fall? (s ii 8)

If we only knew what we were, instead of being astonished at finding ourselves on the ground, we should marvel how we can remain standing up. (lr i 8)

The diversity of paths makes no diversity in ourselves. (lr
ii 14)

We cannot quit ourselves altogether while we are here
below; we must always bear ourselves until God bears us
to heaven. (lw vi 17)

The Philistine only dies with us, and always lives with us.
(t ix 7)

But for holy eternity in which all our days end, we should
have cause to blame our human condition. (lw iii 1)

Natural reason is a good tree which God has planted in us;
the fruits which spring from it cannot but be good. (t xi
1)

There is no nature, though never so good, which may not
be perverted to evil by vicious habits. There is no disposition, though ever so perverse, that may not, by the grace
of God and our own industry, be brought under control
and overcome. (in i 24)

Sometimes we so much occupy ourselves with being good angels that we neglect to be good men and women. (LW I 5)

For you, there are but God and yourself in the world. (LR I 2)

Our imperfection must accompany us to our coffin; we cannot move without touching earth. (LW I 5)

The World

We must make use of this world as though we were making no use of it at all. (S XVI 4)

We should enjoy spiritual things but only use corporal things. (IN III 39)

All the world together is not worth one soul. (IN V 14)

Never look at what the world offers without considering what it hides. (LW I 9)

Let us consider that all we have makes us nothing more than the rest of the world, and that all this is nothing before God. (LW I 2)

In this world there is no wealth without anxiety, no

repose without labor, no consolation without affliction, no health without sickness. (C III)

In this perishable life, good is never to be found without evil following in its train. (C III)

This life presents a continuous variety of diverse accidents. (C III)

We cannot stand well with the world unless we become one with it. (IN IV 1)

The world holds us to be fools; let us hold it to be mad. (IN IV 1)

One cannot perfectly love God unless one forsake affections for perishable things. (T XII 10)

The little affections of *thine* and *mine* are remnants of the world, in which there is nothing so precious. (C VIII)

How often the world calls good what is evil, and still oftener evil what is good! (LW II 30)

Who does not see that the world is an unjust judge; gracious and favorable toward its own children but harsh and rigorous toward the children of God? (IN IV 1)

We may weep a little over this world which is dying, yea, which is dead for us, and to which we mean forever to die. (LR IV 35)

Trouble yourself little about what the world thinks, and let it say what it likes, good or ill. (LW VI 52)

The children of the world are all separated one from another because their hearts are in different places. (LW II 11)

Leave to the worldly their world. (LW I 10)

Eternal Life

Earth is no farther from heaven than the supernatural ways of God from our earthly ways. (S XXI 9)

We are all pilgrims in this mortal life. (T IV 5)

The world is only peopled to people heaven. (LW II 32)

We should really live in this world as though our spirit were already in heaven. (S IV 6)

Little does passing time matter to a soul which aspires to eternity, and which only takes notice of perishing moments in order to pass by them into immortal life. (LR IV 8)

Our hearts have a thirst which cannot be quenched by the pleasures of this mortal life. (T III 10)

This life is short and it is only given us to gain the other. (LW I 1)

The shortest life is the best life if it leads us to the eternal. (LW II 33)

Two or three years soon pass and eternity remains. (LR II 15)

Whoever thinks well on eternity troubles himself little about what happens in these three or four moments of mortal life. (LW VI 54)

We in this life are walking as it were on ice. (C III)

What is not for eternity, can be nothing but vanity. (LW VI 43)

The day that is past must not judge the day present, nor the present day judge that which is past; it is only the Last Day that judges all. (IN III 29)

God's love will be our guerdon in this life, and He Himself will be our reward in eternity. (C XIV)

II

Thou Hast Made
Us For Thee, O God!

God wants you wholly and without reserve, and to the very utmost stripped and denuded of self. (LR V 5)

Amongst all loves, God's is so to be preferred that we must always stand prepared in mind to forsake them all for that alone. (T X 7)

God's Love for Us

How amorous the divine Heart is of our love! (T II 8)

When did God's love for you begin? When He began to be God. When did He begin to be God? Never, for He has always been without beginning and without end, and so He has always loved you from all eternity. (IN V 14)

If God had not created man He would still indeed have been perfect in goodness, but He would not have been actually merciful, since mercy can only be exercised toward the miserable. (C II)

So gentle is God's hand in the handling of our hearts! (T II 12)

God never loves a soul more without bestowing upon her more charity, our love toward Him being the proper and special effect of His love toward us. (T III 2)

There is no great spirit except that of God, who is so good that He willingly dwells in our little spirits. (LR III 30)

The divine Majesty never fails in care or foresight. (C XVII)

God's jealousy of us is not a jealousy of cupidity, but of friendship: our love is useless to Him, but to us a great gain. (T X 13)

No man can ever complain as though the divine Majesty were wanting to anyone. (T II 5)

Who is mad enough to think it possible to sin more than God can forgive? (S VI 3)

Our misery is far less than God's mercy. (S VI 3)

No, no, God is not so terrible to those whom He loves— He is content with little, for He well knows we have not much. (LR I 8)

God does not love our imperfections and venial sins, but

He loves us much in spite of them. (LW VI 48)

The sovereign spirit of God is everywhere, without whose leave no spirit stirs. (LR IV 14)

The world is a great stage on which God displays His many wonders. (S XIX 3)

God is a hidden God and He likes to be served and worshiped secretly. (S VII 11)

God works from afar and from close by, and calls the distant to the service of those who serve Him without bringing them near. (LR IV 15)

God rejects nothing in which no malice or ill-will is to be found. (C XX)

Grace

There is an incomparable correspondence between God and man for their reciprocal perfection. (T I 15)

A little reed in the hand of grace becomes a mighty staff. (S XIV 7)

Nous aspirons à lui, et respirons en lui. (LW IV 27)

We are awake, but have not awakened of ourselves. (T II 10)

Not only is God in the place where you are, but He is in a very special manner in the depth of your spirit. (I II 2)

If we do not repulse the grace of holy love, it dilates itself by continual increase in our souls. (T II 2 1)

The grace of God supplies the void, and where there is less nature there is more grace. (LR V 9)

We must take care that what we do not expect from our strength we do expect from the grace of God. (LW IV 1 3)

One ounce of sanctifying grace is worth more than a hundred pounds of those graces which theologians call "gratuitous," of which the gift of miracles is one. (S V 3)

He who has done you the grace of making the first stroke, will Himself make with you the others; and because His hand is entirely paternal, either will do it insensibly, or if He let you feel it, He will give you the needed constancy and gladness. (LR IV 2 1)

How can the ardour of love possibly make one desire to be separated from grace, since love is grace itself? (T X 1 6)

Spiritual benefits do not inflame us unless we behold the eternal will which destines them for us. (T XII 1 2)

If you lie to the Holy Ghost, it is no wonder He should refuse His consolations. (IN IV 14)

God pours His love no less over one soul, though He loves it with an infinity of others, than if He loved that one only. (T X 14)

Things which God does by a peculiar grace we make too much of an affair of state, and put too much worldly policy into it. (LR III 25)

How often does it happen that we say good things because some good soul gets us the grace to do so! We are like organs, where he who gives the wind really does the whole work and gets no praise for it. (LR VI 5)

When God calls anyone to Christianity He obliges Himself to furnish him with all that is required for being a good Christian. (LR V 8)

Blessed be the wind, whencesoever it comes, that makes us speed to a good port. (LR IV 24)

Desire and Will

We must desire to love and love to desire what can never be enough desired or loved. (LW I 3)

Love celestial desires, and desire celestial love. (LW I 3)

We never desire, with a *true* desire, anything which is not possible. (LW VII 24)

To desire something for any reason than for God is to desire God less. (S I 3)

Desiring to love, the noble spirit receives pain; but loving to desire, he receives sweetness. (T VI 13)

To desire to love God is to love to desire Him, and hence to love Him; for love is the root of all desire. (S I 3)

God only values man for his soul, and the soul only for its will, and the will only for its love. (IN III 18)

The will only loves while willing to love. (T I 4)

The will changes her condition according to the love she espouses. (T I 4)

Christ came to bless good wills, and little by little He will make them fruitful and of good effect. (LR VI 2)

There are no galley slaves in the royal vessel of divine love—every man works his oar voluntarily. (S VII 3)

We have freedom to do good or evil; yet to make choice of evil, is not to use, but to abuse our freedom. (T XII 10)

Grace is so gracious that she in no way offends the liberty of our will. (T II 12)

God presses us but does not oppress our liberty. (T II 12)

God will do your work with you if you will do His work with Him. (LR III 46)

God would never have rejected you if you had not rejected His love. (T II 10)

It is our part to plant and water carefully, but to give increase—that belongs only to God. (T IX 6)

The farmer will never be reprehended for not having a good harvest, but only if he did not carefully till and sow his ground. (T IX 7)

God did not deprive you of the operation of His love, but you did deprive His love of your co-operation. (T II 10)

No creature can take us away by force from holy love; we only can abandon it by our own will. (T III 4)

God does not forsake unless forsaken; He never takes away His gifts till we take away our hearts. (T II 10)

It is the will only that God desires, but all the other powers run after it to be united to God with it. (T VII 2)

Promptitude in doing the will of God is a wonderful means of drawing down great and powerful graces for the accomplishment of every good work. (LR IV 21)

No servant of God can be without this desire: Oh how greatly I wish to serve God better! (LR II 24)

The Love of God

The love of God is the end, the perfection and the excellence of the universe. (T X 1)

The love of God is a love without peer, because the goodness of God is a peerless goodness. (T X 6)

It is the great good of our souls to be "to God," and the greatest good to be *only* "to God." (LW I 16)

The love of men toward God takes its being, progress and perfection from the eternal love of God toward men. (T IV 6)

That which is not God is for us nothing. (LR III 18)

We retire to God because we aspire to Him, and we aspire to Him in order to retire to Him. (IN II 13)

He who most loves will be most loved. (LR III 43)

Charity is a love of friendship. (T II 22)

The love of complacency draws God into our hearts, but the love of benevolence casts our hearts into God. (T VIII 2)

Happy is the heart that loves God without pretense of any other pleasure than that it takes in pleasing God! (T IX 11)

We must seek in God only the love of His beauty, not the pleasure which is in the beauty of this love. (T IX 10)

Truth which is not charitable springs from a charity which is not true. (S II 12)

He who communicates according to the spirit of the Spouse annihilates himself, and says to our Lord: annihilate me and convert me into Thee. (LR IV 12)

God looks at the intention of the heart rather than the gifts He is offered. (S XV 9)

All is made for charity, and charity for God. (T VIII 6)

There is nothing small in the service of God. (LR III 26)

When the house is on fire, people are ready to throw

everything out of the window; when the heart is full of God's love, people are certain to look upon all else as of little worth. (s III 1)

Those whose one desire is to please the divine Lover, have neither inclination nor leisure to turn back upon themselves. (C XII)

How happy are we to be slaves of God, who made Himself a slave for us! (LR II 8)

Charity is the pure gold which makes us rich in eternal wealth. (s V 2)

Charity never enters the heart without lodging there all the other virtues in its train. (IN III 1)

Charity is amongst the virtues, as the sun amongst the stars; she distributes to all their lustre and beauty. (T XI 9)

It is not right to keep the humanity of Jesus Christ and at the same time have this admirable wine of heaven—the Holy Spirit. (LR VI 16)

We must sometimes leave our Lord in order to please others for the love of Him. (LW II 6)

Never does any love take away our hearts from God, save that which is contrary to Him. (T X 3)

Let everything be in confusion, not only around us but even within us, yet always the highest point of our heart must look unceasingly toward the love of God. (I IV 13)

The most certain sign that we love God only in all things is when we love Him equally in all things. (S I 8)

Charity is much stronger and more assiduous than mere natural affection. (C XXI)

We leave charity for a moment, and this imperfect habit of human love is thrust upon us, and we content ourselves with it as if it were true charity, till some clear light shows us that we have been deceived. (T IV 10)

Do much for God, and do nothing without love; apply all to this love; eat and drink for it. (LW III 11)

The Love of Neighbor

To love our neighbor in charity is to love God in man. (T X 11)

Finding God in creatures and creatures in God, great souls love God, not the creatures. (T X 5)

We should always love our neighbor as in the breast of Christ. (s II 1)

Since God is the unity of our hearts, who shall ever separate us? (LR II 14)

We are all brethren, all of one flesh. (s II 15)

Let us live in God and we shall be together. (LR I 6)

We share in the sufferings and death of those we love. (LW II 34)

Charity regards the beauty of the heart and spreads itself over all without distinction. (LR II 25)

We must help one another as much as we can, and leave the rest to God. (LR I 8)

It is a great part of our perfection to support one another in our imperfections. (LR II 22)

Bearing with the imperfections of our neighbor is one of the chief characteristics of our love for him. (C IV)

Do not sow a crop of good intentions in your neighbor's garden, but cultivate your own with diligence. (s XIII 7)

No one gives love voluntarily who does not receive it necessarily. (IN III 18)

It is not for the creature's sake that you submit yourself to the creature, but for the love of the Creator whom you acknowledge in the creature. (LR V 12)

Consideration of others is as much the offspring of charity as fasting is the sister of obedience. (S VIII 11)

It is to those who have the most need of us that we ought to show our love more especially. (C IV)

We desire to be borne with in our miseries and always find them worthy of toleration; those of our neighbor always seem to us greater and heavier to bear. (LR V 13)

Whatever love invites us to do, whether for the rich or for the poor, is equally pleasing to God. (S XII 2)

When charity requires it we must freely and mildly communicate to our neighbor not only what is necessary for his instruction, but also what is profitable for his consolation. (IN III 5)

Love the poor and poverty, for it is by this love that you shall become truly poor. (IN III 15)

Let us treat our servants as ourselves, or rather as we should wish to be treated if we were in their position. (s VII 9)

If you tear out one of my eyes, I shall look at you as my very dear friend with the other. (s II 3)

We can never love our neighbor too much. (c IV)

PART II

I

Beginnings and Ends

Charity is both the means and the end, the one and only way by which we can attain that perfection which in truth is charity itself. (s 1 1)

Perfection

The perfection of charity is the perfection of life, for the life of our soul is charity. (LW VI 52)

Virtue is something positive, not a mere absence of its contrary. (C X)

We can never attain to perfection while we have an affection for any imperfection. (C VIII)

Wheresoever we are, we can and should aspire to a perfect life. (IN 1 3)

When we aim at perfection, we must aim at the center, but we must not be troubled if we do not always hit it. (C IV)

We must not be astonished to see ourselves imperfect,

since we must never see ourselves otherwise in this life. (LR I 2)

We must suffer our imperfection in order to have perfection. (LW I 5)

Do not examine so anxiously whether you are in perfection or not. (LR I 2)

One little fault for which we keep an affection is more contrary to perfection than a hundred others committed inadvertently and without affection. (C VIII)

The person who would attain perfection must bear with his own impatience. (S IX 1)

Perfection does not lie in not seeing the world, but in not tasting or relishing it. (LW VI 52)

We must not want to have all begin with perfection: it matters little how one begins, provided that one is quite resolved to proceed well or to finish well. (LR III 31)

We must take all the care God wishes us to take about perfecting ourselves, and yet leave the care of arriving at perfection entirely to Him. (C III)

Self-Love

Nothing troubles us except self-love. (LR I 8)

We carry self about with us everywhere and frailty is deeply imbedded in our soul. (S XXII 6)

Self-love is cunning, it pushes and insinuates itself into everything, while making us believe it is not there at all. (LR I 1)

The *mine* and *thine* reigns so much the more powerfully in spiritual things because they seem to be a spiritual *mine* and *thine*. (LR III 25)

Self-love often deceives us and leads us away, gratifying its own passions under the name of zeal. (T X 15)

The soul that only loves God for love of herself, loves herself as she ought to love God and God as she ought to love herself. (T II 17)

The Holy Ghost cries everywhere that our ruin is from ourselves. (T IV 5)

That peace which is not willing to be broken is an object of self-love. (LR V 5)

Let yourself be governed by God, think not so much of yourself. (LR I 2)

We are more troublesome to ourselves than anyone else is to us. (LW VI 52)

What are all these things which we quit for God but brief moments of a liberty which is a thousand times worse slavery than slavery itself? (LR IV 21)

Not only can the soul which knows her misery have great confidence in God, but that, unless she has such knowledge, she cannot have true confidence in Him. (C II)

It is no honor to be handsome when a man prizes himself for it. (IN III 4)

We must in no wise live according to human prudence, but according to the faith of the Gospel. (LR III 37)

May we be no longer those old selves that we were formerly, but be other selves! (LR VI 9)

Confession and Sorrow for Sin

The Holy Ghost will have no putting off, but desires great promptitude in obeying His inspirations. (C III)

It is sad to see a precious liquor lose its worth through the presence of a little dirt, and an exquisite wine by the admixture of water. (LR I 1)

Why should we die a spiritual death, since we have so sovereign a remedy at hand? (IN II 19)

As we consider our sins in detail, let us consider God's graces in detail. (IN III 5)

Do not content yourself with confessing your venial sins merely as to the fact, but accuse yourself also of the motive which induced you to commit them. (IN II 19)

The loving heart loves God's commandments; and the harder they are the more sweet and agreeable it finds them. (T VIII 5)

Everyone argues in favor of the virtue which he practices easily, and exaggerates the difficulties of the virtues which are contrary to it. (LR II 25)

It is only weak heads that are made to ache with the scent of roses. (S VIII 3)

The sting of honeybees is more painful than that of other insects. (LR III 16)

If sin abounds in malice to ruin us, grace superabounds to restore us. (T XI 1 2)

Christians are so very wrong to be as little Christian as they are. (LW II 36)

We must be very sorry for faults with a repentance which is strong, constant, tranquil, but not troubled, unquiet or fainthearted. (T IX 7)

What better penance can a heart do which commits faults than to submit to a continual abnegation of self-will? (LR III 8)

Christ was more concerned with St. Peter's repentance and remorse than with his sin. (S VII 8)

We correct ourselves better by a tranquil and steadfast repentance than by that which is harsh, eager and passionate. (IN III 9)

One of the most excellent intentions that we can possibly have in all our actions, is to do them because our Lord did them. (C XVIII)

Lift Up Your Hearts!

Lift up your heart quite tranquilly when it falls, humbling

yourself before God by acknowledging your misery, without being in the least astonished at your fall. (IN III 9)

Live joyously amongst your holy occupations! (LR II 29)

Weep a little now, but moderate your tears and bless God. (LW IV 8)

How happy are they whom God turns as He likes, and leads according to His good pleasure, whether by tribulation or consolation. (LR IV 24)

Nothing but sin should sadden us, and to this sorrow for sin it is necessary that holy joy should be attached. (LR IV 29)

Well! my poor heart, here we are, fallen into the ditch which we had made so firm a resolution to avoid; ah! let us rise and leave it forever. Courage! henceforth let us be more on our guard, God will help us, we shall do well enough! (IN III 9)

The putting down of self must be practiced gently, tranquilly, constantly, and not only sweetly, but gaily and joyously. (LR IV 12)

Even when we are sorry for sin, holy joy should immediately be called to our rescue. (S II 14)

Nothing makes the milk dry up like sadness. (LR III 34)

We may be excused for not always being bright, but we are not excused for not being always gracious, yielding and considerate. (T XI 21)

This equableness of humor, this joy and sweetness of heart, is rarer than perfect chastity; but it is also the more desirable for that. (LR II 25)

On no account give way to sadness, the enemy of devotion. (LR IV 29)

No inequality of events must ever carry away our hearts and minds into inequalities of temper. (C III)

We must never suffer our confusion to be attended with sadness and disquietude. (C II)

Walk joyously as far as you can, and if you do not walk joyously, at least walk courageously and faithfully. (LR I 2)

Our imperfections ought not to displease us, but at the same time they ought not to astonish or discourage us. (S XII 5)

Let us do what we can, and then God will be satisfied. (C XX)

Above all, do not be discouraged! (LR II 20)

How to Die Well

We must leisurely say good-by to the world, and little by little withdraw our affections from creatures. (LW IV 14)

We must live a dying life, and we must die a living death in the life of our Lord. (S XV 6)

In what measure God draws to Himself, one by one, the treasures which our heart has here below, He draws with them our heart itself. (LR IV 18)

Go, dear friend, go into that eternal existence, at the time fixed by the King of eternity; we shall go thither after you. (LW II 32)

Happy are they who, being always on their guard against death, find themselves always ready to die. (LW III 4)

Unhappy is death without the love of Christ; unhappy is love without the death of Christ! (T XII 13)

We are dying little by little; so we are to make our imperfections die with us day by day. (LW I 5)

You will not be separated or divided, for all will go away, and all will stay. (C VI)

Our age is not so delightsome that those who quit it should be much lamented. (LW IV 9)

How can he will to die for God who will not live according to God? (T X 8)

The consolations of this life appear in a moment, and another moment carries them off. (LW III 1)

If purgatory is a species of hell as regards suffering, it is even more a species of paradise as regards heavenly love and sweetness. (S VI 6)

II

Be on Your Guard

This life is a continual warfare and there is no one who can say, I am not attacked. (LR III 48)

We are rarely in this mortal life without many temptations. (T IV 2)

The Spiritual Combat

Our victory does not lie in our not feeling imperfections, but in not consenting to them. (IN I 5)

It is a good sign when the devil makes so much noise and tempest round about the will; it is a sign that he is not within. (LW VI 3)

All the temptations of hell cannot stain a soul which does not love them. (LW VI 6)

To have no bad inclinations does not depend on ourselves, while to have bad affections does. (C VIII)

Let the enemy rage at the gate, let him knock, let him push, let him cry, let him howl, let him do worse; we know for certain that he cannot enter save by the door of our consent. (LR I 8)

When we are assailed by some vice, we must, as far as possible, embrace the practice of the contrary virtue. (IN III 1)

Virtue does not require that we should be deprived of the occasion of falling into the imperfection which is its opposite. (C III)

While the temptation displeases you there is nothing to fear; for why does it displease you, save because you do not will it? (LW VI 3)

You must not reply nor appear to hear what the enemy says; let him clamor as much as he likes at the door; you must not say as much as, Who goes there? (LW III 11)

Our Lord permits us to fail in little occasions, that we may humble ourselves and know that if we have overcome certain great temptations it is not by our own strength. (LR IV 32)

Disquietude is not a mere temptation, but a source from which and through which many temptations come. (IN IV 11)

Have we to avoid evil?—we must do so peacefully. (LR I 8)

We are greatly exposed to temptations when our body is too much pampered, and when it is too much weakened. (IN III 23)

There is nothing so like as two drops of water—yet the one may be from roses, the other from hemlock; one cures, the other kills. (LR I 1)

Fear

We must fear God through love, not love Him through fear. (S I 16)

We are not drawn to God by iron chains, but by sweet attractions and holy inspirations. (T II 12)

Love virtue rather than fear sin. (S XIX 1)

Fear is a greater evil than the evil itself. (LW VI 12)

We must not fear fear. (LW IV 13)

Have no fear: He who has given you the will, He will give you the accomplishing. (LR IV 21)

There is a great difference between the buzzing of a bee and its sting. (s VIII 8)

Let the waves growl and roar all round about your back, but fear not, for God is there. (LR I 10)

Our enemy is a great clatterer, do not trouble yourself at all about him; he cannot hurt you. (LW III 7)

Why do you put yourself in trouble? God is good; He sees very well what you are. (LR III 16)

Let the wind blow, and think not that the rustling of the leaves is the clash of arms. (LW VI 6)

It is not good to walk on tiptoe, either in mind or in body, for if we stumble, the fall is all the worse. (LW I 3)

Those who love to be feared, fear to be loved. (s VII 3)

Let the world turn upside down, let everything be in darkness, in smoke, in uproar—God is with us. (LW VI 12)

The good angels are around you like a company of sentinels on guard. (LR IV 14)

It will be quite enough to receive the evils which come

upon us from time to time, without anticipating them by the imagination. (LR IV 2)

Presumption

Since you have not yet your own wings for flight, do not flutter and do not make eager attempts to fly. (LW VI 2)

We usually know what we ought to do, but we rarely know what we should do; it is always a sign of presumption to imagine ourselves able to handle hot coals without burning ourselves. (S XVI 6)

Our Lord does not wish us to carry His cross except by one end. (C VII)

The providence of God is wiser than we. (LW VI 25)

Even though you may at the present moment feel strength sufficient to endure mortifications and humiliations, how do you know that you will always have it? (C XXI)

Do not desire crosses, save in proportion to the measure wherewith you have borne those that have been already sent you. (IN III 37)

I should not have the courage to ask our Saviour by the pains which He had in His head that I should have none in mine—I would rather use the crowning of our Lord to obtain a crown of patience around my aching head! (LR IV 26)

We must not summon sufferings into our hearts as our Lord did, for we cannot govern them as He did. (LR IV 11)

Huntsmen push into brambles, and often return more injured than the animal they intend to injure. (LW IV 3)

Just walk on uninterruptedly and very quietly; if God makes you run, He will enlarge your heart. (LR V 13)

It is a great folly to wish to be wise with an impossible wisdom. (T 1 3)

You can only give God what you have. (LW II 18)

Rash Judgments

Those who look well after their own consciences rarely fall into the sin of judging others. (S II 15)

If we judge ourselves we will not be judged by God. (S II 14)

To find fault with our neighbor is to admit that we are not

attentive of our responsibility for his wrong actions. (LR II 18)

The business of finding fault is very easy, and that of doing better very difficult. (LR III 1)

We should perhaps have done worse than our fallen neighbor if God did not hold us by the right hand. (S II 8)

It is the part of a futile soul to busy herself with examining the lives of others. (IN III 28)

He who could take away detraction from the world, would take away from it a great part of its sins and iniquities. (IN III 29)

We accuse our neighbor for little, and we excuse ourselves in much. (IN III 36)

Whatever we see our neighbor do we must always interpret his conduct in the best manner possible. (C IV 2)

If it were possible for a neighbor's action to have a hundred different aspects, we should look at it in that aspect which is most favorable. (IN III 28)

Support and greatly excuse your neighbor with great sweetness of heart. (LR V 1)

My tongue, while I speak of my neighbor, is in my mouth, like a lancet in the hand of the surgeon who wishes to make an incision between the nerves and the sinews. (IN III 29)

When we cannot excuse the sin, at all events let us make it worthy of compassion, by attributing to it the most extenuating cause which it can have, such as ignorance or infirmity. (IN III 28)

Since the goodness of God is so great that one single moment suffices to obtain and receive His grace, what assurance can we have that a man who was a sinner yesterday is so today? (IN III 29)

Do not accuse or excuse yourself without proper consideration; if you accuse yourself without reason, you will become a coward, and if you excuse yourself without reason, you will become overconfident. (S XIV 3)

III

Man's True Calling

God has many ways of calling His servants to Himself. (LR v 8)

In the creation God commanded the plants to bring forth their fruits each one after its kind. (IN 1 3)

Vocation

A good vocation is simply a firm and constant will which the called person has to serve God in the way and in the places to which Almighty God has called him. (LR v 8)

How foolish are those who waste time and thought in desiring to be martyred in the Indies, but do not apply themselves to the duties of their state of life! (C VII)

Walk ever in the way of your vocation with simplicity, more intent on doing than on desiring; that is the shortest road. (C IX)

The love of our parents, friends and benefactors is in itself according to God, yet we may love them in excess; as also our vocations, be they ever so spiritual. (T X 4)

God Himself will uphold you with the same hand with which He placed you in this vocation. (LR III 8)

Any devotion which is in opposition to, or not in conformity with, man's true calling is not an authentic devotion. (S XXI 3)

Genuine devotion is consistent with every state of life. Like liquid poured into a container, it adapts itself to any shape. (S XXI 3)

Necessary employments, according to each one's vocation, do not diminish Divine love, but increase it. (T XII 5)

Let Martha be active without criticizing Mary, let Mary contemplate without despising Martha, for our Lord will always take the part of the one who is censured. (S XXI 9)

When charity draws some to poverty and withdraws others from it, when she directs some to marriage and others to continence, when she shuts one up in a cloister and makes another quit it, she is not bound to give an account thereof to anyone. (T VIII 6)

We must consider that there is no vocation which has not its irksomenesses, its bitternesses, and disgusts. (LW II 4)

God makes the lame and the blind to come to His banquet, to show us that two eyes and two legs are not needed for going to Paradise. (LR V 8)

In order to have signs of a good vocation, it is not necessary to possess visible constancy, but it must reign effectively in the higher will. (C XVII)

Make a virtue of necessity. (IN III 16)

If a person shows a firm and persevering determination to serve God in the manner and place to which His divine Majesty calls her, she gives the best proof we can have that she has a true vocation. (C XVII)

Neither widowhood nor virginity has any place in heaven but that which is assigned to them by humility. (IN III 40)

While one is busying oneself to seek out what very often is not one's vocation, one omits what would render us perfect in that which we have embraced. (LR V 8)

We must love what God loves; now He loves our vocation. (LW II 4)

Marriage

It is a happy thing when two souls meet who love each other only in order to love God better. (LR IV 1)

What God unites cannot be separated. (LR IV 15)

If the glue is good, two pieces of fir glued together will cleave so fast to each other that they can be more easily broken in any other place than where they were joined. (IN III 38)

Love equalizes lovers. (T V 5)

The state of marriage is one which requires more virtue and constancy than any other; it is a perpetual exercise of mortification. (LW I 8)

Marriage is an order in which the profession must be made before the novitiate. (S VII 10)

As for those who are married, chastity consists not in abstaining absolutely from carnal pleasures, but in restraining themselves in the midst of pleasures. (IN III 12)

How agreeable to God are the virtues of a married woman! (LW II 8)

The well-being of a household depends on the parents' words, but far more on their behavior. (S XXII 10)

The home is not a convent. (S XXI 6)

The closest and most fruitful union between husband and wife is that which is effected in holy devotion. (IN III 38)

He that does not wish to receive lodgers should take down the signboard from his house. (IN III 25)

The Care of Souls

There is no soil so barren but that diligent tenderness brings forth some fruit. (S II 13)

The most perfect care is that which approaches nearest to the care which God has of us, which is a care full of peace and quietness, and which in its highest activity has still no emotion. (LR IV 27)

It is not a good excuse to say: I have no breasts, I have no milk; for it is not with our own milk or our own breasts that we feed the children of God. (LR III 46)

There are many good doctors who are far from being in good health, and there are many beautiful paintings made by ugly painters. (LR IV 1)

The care of souls is as a burden of sweet cinnamon, which, by its invigorating scent, revives those who bear it. (S XXII 8)

A very impure soul can attain a perfect purity if well assisted. (LR V 6)

Do the Seraphim despise the little Angels, do the great saints despise the less? (LR III 43)

He who seeks only the glory of God finds it in poverty as in abundance. (LR III 15)

Remember that the practice of devotion must be adapted to the strength, the employment, and the duties of each one in particular. (IN I 3)

We must not marvel that each herb and flower in a garden requires its special care. (LR II 23)

Do not require more perfection from others than from yourself. (LR I 2)

Be more indulgent toward others and more disciplinary with yourself. (S VII 2)

True zeal pardons certain things, or at least winks at them until the appropriate time and place for correcting them. (S VII 7)

If you press a man, you oppress him; if you oppress him, you irritate him; if you irritate him, you lose hold of him. (S XX 4)

Admonition is naturally bitter, but when mixed with the sugar of loving-kindness, and warmed by the fire of charity, it becomes acceptable, gracious and very cordial. (s ii 13)

One can catch more flies with a spoonful of honey than with a hundred barrels of vinegar. (s ii 13)

Love is a magistrate who exercises his authority without noise, without policemen or sergeants. (T viii 1)

Do you know how I test the value of a preacher? If the listeners go away striking their breasts, saying: "Today I will do better"; not by their saying: "What a wonderful sermon." (s xix 12)

The remonstrances of a father given gently and affectionately have much more power to correct the child than those which are given angrily and wrathfully. (IN iii 8)

We must fight back with affection and not with reason. (LW iii 11)

What you see can be done with love you must do; what can only be done with debate must be left alone. (LW ii 10)

He who preaches with love preaches sufficiently against

heretics, though he say not a single word of controversy against them. (LW VI 59)

One single good work done with a tranquil spirit is worth far more than several done with eagerness. (C VII)

All the defects which occur in a good work do not spoil its essential goodness; wherever good comes from we must love it. (LR IV 23)

The Religious Life

There is nothing so blessed as a devout religious, nothing so miserable as a religious without devotion. (LR I 4)

Since you cannot be in real solitude, be in mental solitude. (LR VI 28)

Religious Orders are not formed for the purpose of gathering together perfect people, but those who have the courage to aim at perfection. (C XVI)

When God calls anyone to be a religious, He binds Himself to bestow on that person all that is needed for perfection in his vocation. (C XVII)

We must not think that in entering Religion one becomes perfect all of a sudden, but that one enters there to tend to perfection. (LR V 8)

The religious life is not a natural life; it is above nature, and its soul is given and formed by grace. (LR IV 20)

It is God, and not the cell, that we must choose for our dwelling place. (S XXII 5)

As religious who have left the world ought to wish never to see it again, so the world which has left them never wants to see them again. (LR I 11)

We must bear with this inconvenience of the love of our relations and friends who think there is no comparison between the satisfaction of being with them and that which is found in the course of God's service. (LR VI 28)

Those who desire to live according to nature should stay in the world, and only those should enter Religion who are determined to live according to grace. (C XX)

Do not attach yourself to anything so much as to the religious rules, so that you go where the rules draw you. (LR V 2)

One can be a good religious without reciting in choir, without wearing this or that particular habit, without abstinence from such or such things; but without poverty and community of goods, no one can be so. (LR I 1)

It is no use to say *our* veil, *our* dress, *our* tunic, or *our* linen, if in fact the use of them is not indifferent and common to all. (LR IV 6)

There are evil spirits who go to and fro in desert places quite as much as in cities. (S XXII 6)

Let not yourself be misled by past errors, or of future hardships in this crucified life of religion. (LW I 19)

Bees from time to time quit their hive, but only from necessity or for purpose of utility, returning to it as quickly as possible. (C XVI)

The religious who has begun well has not done all, unless he perseveres even to the end. (C XI)

Friendship

To those who find the doors of religion as well as of marriage closed to them, a holy friendship is nigh indispensable for the welfare of their souls. (LW IV 53)

The friendship of well-regulated souls is extremely useful to us to keep our own well-regulated. (LW IV 2)

Perfection does not consist in having no friendships at all, but in having that which is good, holy and sacred. (IN III 19)

What is there to be loved and desired if friendship is not! (T III 13)

Heaven and earth are not distant enough to separate the hearts which our Lord has joined. (LR II 18)

Friendship pours out its grace upon all the actions of him who is loved, however little ground of favor there may be. (T XI 2)

How far more constant are the friendships founded in charity than those whose foundation is in flesh and blood. (LW I 6)

Friendship requires the exchange of good, not evil. (IN III 22)

The bitternesses of friends are sweets. (T XI 2)

We must love our friends notwithstanding their imperfections, but we must not love their imperfections. (IN III 22)

The friendship which ends in fine words is not of great worth. (C IV 1)

Mere earthly friendships are not apt to last, their origin being so frail that the slightest contradiction chills them. (S II 1)

Friendship which could never end was never true. (LW VII 20)

Friendships begun in this world will be taken up again, never to be broken off. (LW III 4)

You know the spot where our hearts meet—there they can see one another in spite of the distance of places. (LR I 8)

Never think that distance of place can ever separate souls which God has united by the ties of His Love. (LW II 11)

It is absolutely necessary for friendship that reciprocity should exist between the two who love each other, and that this friendship should be contracted through the action of reason. (C IV)

Change of scene is a very great help to alleviate the heat and restlessness, whether of sorrow or of love. (IN III 21)

There is nothing like separation of dwellings to preserve union of hearts between those of opposite, although good, characters and aims. (LW III 9)

PART III

I

The Little Virtues

Occasions are not often presented for the exercise of fortitude, magnanimity and great generosity; but simplicity, humility and gentleness are virtues wherewith all the actions of our life should be tempered. (IN III 1)

Let us practice certain little virtues proper for our littleness. (LW I 5)

Simplicity

There is no artifice as good and desirable as simplicity. (IN III 30)

Simplicity always follows the rule of the love of God. (C XII)

Holy simplicity does not run after its words and actions, but leaves the result of them to divine Providence. (C XII)

Do not examine your soul so much about its advancement. (LR III 16)

The pilgrim who spends all his time counting his steps will make little headway. (S XII 3)

Walk simply, do not desire repose of spirit too earnestly, and you will have the more of it. (LR III 16)

I recommend to you holy simplicity: look before you, and regard not those dangers which you see afar off. (LW I 5)

Those who run best in the race do not think of the crowd which is looking at them. (LW IV 1)

The nightingale loves her melody no less when she makes her pauses than when she sings; the devout heart loves love no less when she turns to exterior necessities than when she prays. (T XII 5)

Great works lie not always in our way, but every moment we may do little ones with excellence, that is, with great love. (T XII 6)

If humility prevents me from playing the wise man, simplicity will likewise prevent me from playing the fool. (IN III 5)

If the prudence of the serpent be not tempered with the simplicity of the dove of the Holy Spirit, it is altogether poisonous. (LR III 42)

The grace of concealing a grace is in itself not slight. (S VIII 11)

Be neat, but be on your guard against affectation, vanity and singularity. (IN III 25)

The man who makes false excuses actually accuses himself most forcibly; but the man who accuses himself in true simplicity deserves to be mercifully excused. (S XIV 3)

In everything I love simplicity. (LR I 1)

Humility

Humility is a descending charity and charity is an ascending humility. (S VIII 1)

Do not desire not to be what you are, but desire to be very well what you are. (LW VI 19)

He who stays not in his littleness, loses his greatness. (LR III 43)

Annihilate yourself in the very depths of your being, to see that God wills to use your littleness to do Him a service of great importance. (LR V 6)

Let us sweetly hide our littleness in His greatness. (LR III 28)

Humble yourself lovingly before God and men, for God speaks to ears bowed down. (LR III 19)

The highest point of humility is not only to know one's abjection, but to love it. (LW VI 1 2)

A man who despises himself in true humility is happy to discover others who agree with him. (S XIX 3)

Shall I be humble? Yes, if you will it. But I will it. You are it then. But I feel distinctly that I am not. So much the better, for this serves to make it more certain. (LR IV 2 5)

What is the good of making a gilded frame for a paper picture? (LR III 2 1)

We oftentimes approach closer to our Lord by withdrawing through humility than by approaching at our own choice. (LR III 45)

When you humble yourselves, it must be with a gentle and peaceful, not with a querulous and impatient, humility. (C IX)

The more pains holy humility costs you, the more graces it will give you. (LR I 1 8)

Let us never make a show of wishing to be last, unless in our hearts we wish to be such. (IN III 5)

Abase yourself very often in the abyss of your nothingness. (LR V 5)

Self-dispraise is no more than a tricky kind of boasting. (s VIII 3)

True humility makes no pretense of being humble, and scarcely ever utters words of humility. (IN III 5)

You must lovingly leave some work to others, and not seek to have all the crowns. (LR II 6)

Give attention to cutting off your own will, and you will soon quit these phantoms of sanctity in which you repose so superstitiously. (LR III 8)

Provided that God be glorified, we must not care by whom. (C VIII)

He who believes himself to be far advanced in the spiritual life has not even made a good beginning. (s XIII 5)

Patience

Have patience with all the world, but first of all with yourself. (LW VI 17)

The drones make more noise and are in a greater hurry than the bees, but they do not make the honey. (IN III 10)

Things which grow in one day, decay in another. (LR I 6)

Those who aim at the love of God need patience with themselves even more than with others. (S IX 1)

The virtue of patience is the one which most assures us of perfection. (LW I 5)

We always do a thing quickly enough when we do it well. (IN III 10)

The angels have a care for our salvation and procure it with diligence, yet they do not have solicitude, worry and anxiety. (IN III 10)

We must suffer with patience the delay in our perfection, while ever cheerfully doing what we can for our advancement therein. (C X)

Let us await our advancement with patience, and instead of disquieting ourselves because we have so little profited in the time past, let us diligently endeavor to do better in the time to come. (T IX 7)

Have patience to walk with short steps till you have wings to fly. (LR III 19)

Do not be eager about your work. (IN III 10)

Eagerness is the mother-imperfection of all imperfections. (LR I 2)

We shall always have quite soon enough what we desire whenever it pleases God to give it to us. (C X)

Be patient not only in regard to the substance of the afflictions which befall you, but also in regard to the accidental inconveniences which are attached to them. (IN III 3)

It is a sorrowful thing to see how little we imitate the patience of our Saviour. (C XXI)

Obedience

In obedience all is secure; out of it all is to be suspected. (T VIII 1 3)

Some find that there is disobedience in the thing which they desire, and wish that it was not there; others seek for it, and only desire the thing because it is forbidden. (C I)

To find the Saviour outside obedience is to lose Him altogether. (LR VI 2 2)

When God puts inspirations into a heart, the first He gives is obedience. (T VIII 1 3)

You do not receive true remedies by your choice nor through sensible feeling, but through obedience and by reason. (LR IV 3 3)

What greater austerity can there be than to keep one's will in subjection and continual obedience? (LR III 8)

The devil does not fear austerity but holy obedience. (LR III 8)

If, before my body bows to my superior, I have not made an act of inward reverence by humbly willing to submit to him, at least let me take care that this willing reverence accompany the outward gesture. (C I)

The obedience which you pay to the doctor when ill is extremely agreeable to God. (LR I 9)

In proportion to our affection and esteem for the maker of the law, is the exactness of our observance of it. (C XIII)

Do not look into the face of one who governs you, but into the face of God who has so ordained it. (LR V 12)

Rest from obedience, and your repose is more meritorious and more pleasing to God than voluntary labor. (C XI)

If the spiritual attraction comes from God, it will without doubt lead one to obedience. (C XX)

Blessed are the obedient, for God will never suffer them to go astray. (IN III 11)

Gentleness

The spirit of God, gentle, ever sweet, is in the soft refreshing zephyrs, not in the whirlwind, or the tempest. (s xx 4)

Nothing is so strong as gentleness—nothing so loving and gentle as strength. (s iv 9)

Nothing appeases an enraged elephant so much as the sight of a little lamb. (in iii 8)

Who can be angry with those whose only weapons are pearls and diamonds? (s ii 1 3)

The human mind is so constituted that it hardens itself against severity, but loving-kindness makes it pliable. (s ii 1 3)

It often happens in the sittings of parliament, that the ushers crying out "silence" make more noise than those whom they command to be silent. (in iii 8)

It takes more oil than vinegar to make a good salad. (s ii 1 3)

When you encounter difficulties and contradictions, do

not try to break them, but bend them with gentleness and time. (LR I 6)

He who can preserve gentleness amid pains, and peace amid the worry and multitude of affairs, is almost perfect. (LR II 25)

It is always dangerous to take strong remedies. (IN III 12)

Many commit a great fault who are annoyed at having been annoyed, vexed at having been vexed. (IN III 9)

All is gentle to the gentle, and all is holy to the holy. (LR VI 28)

When we discover that our lute is out of tune, we must neither break the strings nor throw the instrument aside. (S IX 2)

The prayer which is made against anger, when it is present and pressing us, must be made gently, tranquilly, without any violence. (IN III 8)

I recommend to you above all the spirit of gentleness. (LR I 5)

Fidelity

As a plant often transplanted can never take root, so the soul that transplants her heart from design to design cannot do well. (T VIII 11)

We must love the holy will of God in little and in great changes. (LR II 11)

Be no less brave for being a Christian, and no less Christian for being brave; and for this we must be very good Christians. (LW IV 2)

What is the use of building castles in Spain, when we have to live in France? (LW VI 19)

That peace is not good which flies the labor required for the glorification of God's name. (LR III 46)

The abjections most profitable to the soul are those which come to us accidentally, or by our own condition of life, because we have not chosen them ourselves. (IN III 6)

We must be faithful in little occasions to obtain fidelity in great ones. (LR IV 29)

He who watches out for his pennies and farthings, will be

still more careful regarding crowns and pounds. (LW IV 53)

It is a little thing to please God in what pleases us: filial fidelity requires that we will to please Him in what does not please us. (LW I 2)

To love God in sugar—little children would do as much; but to love Him in wormwood, that is the test of our fidelity. (LW V 5)

They who wish to live happily and in perfect fidelity, must accustom themselves to live according to reason, rule and obedience, not according to their own inclinations. (C I)

As to your way, God who has guided you up to the present, will guide you to the end. (LR III 16)

Most of the faults committed by good people arise from their not sufficiently keeping a steadfast recollection of the presence of God. (S IV 5)

We have too many aims and designs: we would have the merits of Calvary and the consolations of Thabor both together. (LR III 21)

II

Equilibre Surnaturel

Moderation is always good in all exercises, except in that of loving God. (LR III 20)

This is the height of virtue: to correct immoderation moderately. (LW IV 3)

Spiritual Training

He who aspires to heavenly love, must sedulously reserve for it his leisure, his spirit and his affections. (T XII 3)

To train a young horse to his paces, and to make him steady under his saddle and bridle, takes whole years. (LR IV 19)

Great fires are increased by the wind, but little ones are extinguished, if they be not well protected from it. (IN III 34)

Nothing is more bitter than fruit that is unripe, but when it is preserved, it is sweet and very tasty. (S II 13)

The man who knows best how to control his natural inclinations is more open to supernatural inspirations. (S XV 8)

A life of lower level may be gained in a year, but the perfection to which we aspire cannot come till after many years. (LR IV 16)

Always be correcting yourself of something. (LR II 21)

Do as the bees do: suck honey from all flowers and herbs. (LR I 2)

The enemy is glad to make you lose time when he cannot make you lose eternity. (LR II 13)

A person should never omit his spiritual exercises and the common rules of virtue unless he sees the will of God on the other side. (LW III 11)

We must not strive to practice many exercises at once, for the enemy often tries to make us undertake many designs, to the end that, overwhelmed with the multiplicity of business, we may accomplish nothing. (T VIII 11)

There are all sorts of herbs in a garden, and although there may be one there more excellent than all the others, it does not mean that we are to put no other into the pot. (C X)

The easiest ways do not always lead us the most directly nor the most safely. (LR II 37)

We must be prepared to see weeds growing in our garden and also have the courage to pull them up. (C IX)

Observe God's ways and not your own! (LR V 4)

True love scarcely goes by method. (LR IV 9)

Devotion has no wish to drag others in its train, but simply, humbly and calmly pursues its own road. (C I)

Would you walk in earnest toward devotion? Seek some good man who will guide you; this is the greatest of all words of advice. (IN I 4)

Good advice ought to be well received whether steeped in gall or preserved in honey. (LR I 1)

Choose some particular saints, whose lives you can best appreciate and imitate, and in whose intercession you may have a particular confidence. (IN II 16)

The beginning of good things is good, the progress better, the end the best. (T II 19)

Mount Calvary is the academy of love. (T XII 13)

Liberty of Spirit

Blessed are the hearts which can bend; they shall never be broken. (S VII 1)

The mind must be persuaded, it cannot be constrained. (S XX 4)

We must do all by love, and nothing by force. We must love obedience rather than fear disobedience. (LW III 11)

Constraint is a certain want of liberty by which the soul is overwhelmed with either disgust or anger, when it cannot do what it has planned, though still able to do better. (LW III 11)

A horse that is shackled or tethered cannot run. (LR I 4)

Liberty of spirit is a detachment of the Christian heart from all things to follow the known will of God. (LW III 11)

I leave you the spirit of liberty—not that which excludes obedience, for that is the liberty of the flesh; but that which excludes constraint, scruple and worry. (LW III 11)

Our minds must not be kept always on the stretch. (C IV 1)

Have a holy liberty of spirit about the *means* of perfection.
(LW III 5)

A soul which has true liberty of spirit will leave its exercises with an equal countenance, and a heart gracious toward the importunate person who has inconvenienced her. (LW III 11)

One must not be so devoted to even the most pious practices as to be unable to break into them. (S VIII 11)

We have only to take care not to use a superfluous attention when we seek out the will of God in all the particular details of small, ordinary and trifling actions. (LR V 2)

There is no annoyance so great as the annoyance which is composed of many trifling, but continuous worries. (LR IV 32)

I do not approve that your will should be anticipated by firm resolutions, but only by sweet attractions. (LW III 11)

You were never told not to think about your advancement, but that you were not to think about it anxiously. (C XII)

Let your superior part bear the disorder of the inferior. (LW II 17)

Do not be so anxiously solicitous for Him, for He told Martha that He was better pleased that there should be no solicitude, not even in doing good. (LR III 11)

We must not be unjust and require from ourselves what is not in ourselves. (LW II 17)

The good which is true fears not to be lessened by the increase of other true goods. (LR III 25)

Little by Little

We are little chicks, and have not our wings yet. (LW I 5)

Our arms are not yet long enough to reach the cedars of Lebanon; let us content ourselves with the hyssop of the valleys. (LW VI 7)

Let us leave the lofty heights to the souls who have been raised so high; we shall be only too happy to serve Him in His kitchen and pantry. (IN III 2)

Let us go by land, since the high sea makes our head turn. (LW I 5)

Better is the possession of a small treasure found than the expectation of a greater which is to find. (T VIII 12)

Let us not be troubled at finding ourselves always novices

in the exercise of virtues, for in the monastery of a devout life everyone considers himself always a novice. (T IX 7)

While we are busy and anxious to find out what is the better, we unprofitably let slip the time for doing many good things. (T VIII 14)

To advance well we must apply ourselves to make good way in the road nearest to us, and do the first day's journey. (LW I 5)

We must sometimes take a step back to get a better spring. (LW II 6)

We must not busy ourselves with wanting to do the last day's journey, but remember that we are to do and work out the first. (LW I 5)

Soon enough, if well enough. (S II 8)

It is a well-regulated mixture of both sugar and salt which produces a good flavor in a salad dressing. (S XVII 3)

A sensible mind is a medium mind, which is neither too great nor too little. (LR V 9)

Those who wish to straighten a young tree, not only bring it to the direction in which they wish it to grow, but even bend it somewhat beyond, so that it may not return to its former direction. (C IX)

Salt and sugar are both excellent things, but too much of either spoils the dish. (S XIX 2)

If you must go to excess on one or the other side, let it be toward indulgence, for no sauce was ever spoiled by sugar. (S II 13)

Dying to Self

May we be annihilated in ourselves to live wholly to God! (LR II 1)

We do not become perfect by the multiplication of exercises, penances and austerities, but rather by the purity of love with which we do them. (C XIII)

The crosses that we shape for ourselves are always lighter than the ones laid upon us. (S X 11)

We do not love crosses unless they are in gold, with pearls and enamel. (LW I 10)

Devout souls find much bitterness in their exercises of mortification; but in performing them they convert them into the most delicious sweetness. (IN I 2)

How agreeable to God should we be, if we knew how to use properly the subjects of mortification which our vocation affords. (LW II 18)

To cure the itch there is not so much need to wash and bathe ourselves as to purify the blood. (IN III 23)

It is not right all at once to show strong signs of this death to our natural passion. (LR II 3)

We have not to carry the cross of others, but our own. (LW II 4)

Behold a quantity of crosses and mortifications which you have neither chosen nor wished; receive them, love them! (LW V 2)

It is a thousand times better to die with our Lord than to live without Him. (LW VI 21)

Brother Ass

It is far better to mortify the body through the spirit, than the spirit through the body. (S XV 4)

The devil does not trouble himself much about us if, while macerating our bodies, we are at the same time doing our own will. (S XV 4)

The spirit cannot tolerate the body when overfed, and if underfed, the body cannot tolerate the spirit. (s xv 7)

I approve your keeping Brother Ass subdued, not so much by the abstinence from meats, as by abstinence from choice in them. (LW III 11)

Do not flatter your body by delicacies in eating, sleeping, and such other softnesses. (LW IV 2)

A continual and moderate sobriety is better than immoderate abstinences practiced from time to time. (IN III 23)

Softness of the mind is infinitely more dangerous than that of the body, inasmuch as the mind, being the nobler part, the disease is more difficult to cure. (C XVII)

Abstinence which is practiced against obedience takes away the sin from the body to put it in the heart. (LR III 9)

So long as the enemy can enter our souls and torment us, he does not care how much we mortify our bodies. (s xv 3)

We are far too tender over our bodies, but incomparably more so as regards our souls. (C III)

As long as he who fasts, fasts for God, and he who fasts not, also fasts not for God, devotion is as well satisfied with one as with the other. (C I)

Misery of Mind and Body

Make sickness itself a prayer. (LW II 3 1)

What do you think the bed of tribulation is? It is simply the school of humility. (LR I 8)

God never permits anything to come upon us as a trial or test of our virtue without desiring that we should profit by it. (C XVII)

Our misery is the throne of God's mercy. (LW VI 1 2)

To love sufferings and afflictions for the love of God is the supreme point of most holy charity, for there is nothing therein to receive our affection save the will of God only. (T IX 2)

It is not enough to be afflicted because God wills it; but we must be so as He wills it, when He wills, for as long as He wills, and exactly in the manner in which it pleases Him. (C XXI)

If it be God's will that the remedies overcome the sickness, return to Him thanks with humility; but if it be His will that the sickness overcome the remedies, bless Him with patience. (IN III 3)

Look at afflictions in themselves, and they are dreadful; behold them in the will of God, and they are love and delights. (T IX 2)

God's will is as much in sickness as in health. (T IX 10)

The truly loving heart loves God's good pleasure not in consolations only, but, and especially, in afflictions also. (T IX 2)

Many would be willing to have afflictions provided that they be not inconvenienced by them. (IN III 3)

Desire to grow well, so that you may serve Him, but do not refuse to continue sick, that you may obey Him, and dispose yourself for death, if it be His pleasure, that you may praise Him. (IN III 3)

One ounce of patient suffering is worth far more than a pound of action. (S IX 9)

Long illnesses are good schools of mercy for those who tend the sick, and of loving patience for those who suffer. (S IX 7)

If done lovingly, there is no danger in complaining, nor in begging cure of your illness; only do this with love. (LW II 18)

If you cannot easily communicate often really, you can communicate as often as you like spiritually. (LR VI 19)

Disquietude arises from an inordinate desire to be delivered from the will which we experience, or to obtain the good for which we hope. (IN IV 11)

Take care of your health, that it may serve you to serve God. (LR I 12)

The Poor in Spirit

Practice poverty of spirit in the midst of riches; practice richness of spirit in real poverty. (IN III 14)

Take from your house what is in excess, and add to it what is wanting. (LR I 1)

He is rich in spirit who has his riches in his spirit or his spirit in his riches; he is poor in spirit who has no riches in his spirit, nor his spirit in his riches. (IN III 14)

How much more desirable a thing it is to be poor in the house of God, than to dwell in the palaces of kings. (LW VII 21)

To desire to be poor, but not to be inconvenienced by

poverty, is to desire the honor of poverty and the convenience of riches. (IN III 16)

It is a dangerous thing for mortification and humility to make their abode in wealth. (S XVI 6)

The virtues which grow in prosperity are generally delicate and weakly. (LW III 10)

Renouncements must be made quite gently, simply, and as if one made them for love and not from necessity of the struggle. (LR IV 18)

Be not ashamed to be poor, or to take alms in charity. (IN III 16)

Riches prick us with a thousand troubles in getting them, as many cares in preserving them, and with yet more anxieties in spending them, and with grief in losing them. (S XVI 4)

Peace is better than a fortune. (LW II 10)

III

Prayer

Prayer must be loved, but it must be loved for the love of God. (LR III 44)

There is much to fear in exalted methods of prayer, but one can walk securely in the more common. (LR V 6)

Recollection of the Mind

The desire we have to obtain divine love makes us meditate, but love obtained makes us contemplate. (T VI 3)

Your way is good and there is nothing to object to, save that you go on considering your steps too much, for fear of falling. (LR III 16)

Meditation produces good movements in the will or loving part of our soul. (IN II 6)

If you have the gift for mental prayer, always reserve for that the principal place above private vocal prayers. (IN II 1)

In striving to raise our reasonings too high in divine things by curiosity we grow empty in our thoughts, and instead of arriving at the knowledge of truth, we fall into the folly of our vanity. (T IV 7)

It is better to sleep upon the sacred breast than to watch elsewhere, wherever it be. (T VI 8)

The grace of meditation cannot be gained by any effort of the mind; but there must be a gentle and humble perseverance. (LR I 9)

If in prayer the Holy Spirit gives you the affection before the consideration, you should not make the consideration, since it is only made to stir up the affection. (IN II 8)

Spend an hour in meditation every day. (IN II 1)

Holy Church does not teach us to pray for ourselves in particular, but always for ourselves and for our Christian brethren. (LW III 11)

Always say *we* and *us*, as our Lord has taught us in the *Pater Noster*, in which there is no *mine*, or *my*, or *me*. (C XVIII)

Let all meditations on "the last four things" end always with hope and confidence. (LR I 6)

Consider what God is doing and what you are doing. (IN II 12)

If it please God to give us affections without reasonings and considerations, it is for us a great grace. (LR IV 9)

If while saying your private vocal prayers, you feel your heart drawn to interior prayer, do not resist the attraction. (IN II 1)

Recollection of the Heart

Recollection of the heart is not made by the preparation of love, but by love itself. (T V 7)

The chief exercise of prayer is to speak to God and to hear God speak in the bottom of our heart. (T VI 1)

Always distinguish clearly between the workings of the higher part of your soul and those of the lower. (C XIV)

The sacred gift of prayer is already in the right hand of the Saviour; as soon as ever you shall have emptied yourself of self, He will pour it into your heart. (LR III 19)

He who in praying to God notices that he is praying, is not perfectly attentive to prayer. (T IX 10)

The best prayer is that which keeps us so well employed in God that we think not of ourselves or of what we are doing. (LR IV 9)

If you reflect and bring your eyes backward upon yourself to see how you look when you look upon God, it is not now He that you behold but your own behavior—yourself. (T IX 10)

There are souls who cannot pause and fix their thoughts on any special mystery, being attracted to a certain simplicity which keeps them in perfect tranquillity before God, with no other consideration than the knowledge that they are before Him and that He is their only Good. (C XVIII)

In prayer of quiet, the contentment of the will is to admit no other contentment but that of being without contentment for the love of the good pleasure of its God. (T VI 11)

The height of love's ecstasy is to have our will not in its own contentment but in God's. (T VI 11)

What good does a soul get from being ravished unto God by prayer, if in its conversation and life it is ravished away by earthly, low and natural affections? (LW VI 57)

When we see a soul that has raptures in prayer and yet no ecstasy in her life, these raptures are exceedingly doubtful and dangerous. (T VII 7)

There was never a saint but has had the ecstasy of life and operation. (LW VI 57)

He who in his rapture has more light in the understanding to admire God, than heat in the will to love Him, is to stand upon his guard. (T VII 6)

If the ecstasy of love be more beautiful than good, more bright than warm, more speculative than affective, it is deserving of suspicion. (T VII 6)

The secret of secrets in prayer is to follow attractions in simplicity of heart. (LR IV 9)

Think no more about the unity which God has made in you, nor your heart, nor your soul, nor anything whatsoever. (LR III 6)

Distractions

The smallest distraction does not withdraw your soul from God, for nothing withdraws us from God but sin. (C IX)

Wolves and bears are certainly more dangerous than flies, but they do not cause us so much annoyance, nor do they exercise our patience so much. (IN IV 8)

Flies do not trouble us with their strength, but by their number. (IN III 10)

We fight the monsters of Africa in imagination, and from lack of attention we allow ourselves in reality to be killed by the little serpents that lie in our way. (IN III 37)

We want our prayer to be steeped in orange-flower water, and we would be virtuous in eating sugar. (LR I 8)

Do not permit your spirit to consider its miseries, let God work; He will make something good of it. (LR III 10)

The very solicitude we have not to be distracted causes oftentimes a very great distraction. (T IX 10)

Accustom yourself to know how to pass from prayer to all sorts of actions which your vocation justly and lawfully requires of you. (IN II 8)

It is quite certain that our prayer will be none the less pleasing to God, nor less useful to ourselves for having been made with difficulty. (C XVIII)

When your heart is wandering and distracted, bring it back gently and quietly to its point, restore it tenderly to its Master's side. (LR V 13)

We must be resolutely determined never to give up prayer for any difficulty that we may encounter in it. (C XVIII)

If you did nothing the whole of your hour but bring back your heart patiently and put it near your Lord again, and every time you put it back it turned away again, your hour would be well employed. (LR V 13)

Spiritual Dryness

There is a difference between possessing the presence of God and having the feeling of His presence. (C IX)

If God has stripped you of the sense of His presence, it is in order that even His presence may no longer occupy your heart, but Himself. (LR III 5)

One single act done with dryness of spirit is worth more than many done with sensible devotion. (C VII)

He is always the same God, as worthy to be served in dryness as in consolation. (C III)

There is a great difference between being occupied with God who gives us the contentment, and being busied with the contentment which God gives us. (T VI 10)

It is the supreme point of holy religion to be content with naked, dry, insensible acts, exercised by the superior will alone. (LR II 8)

Look at the bees upon the thyme; they find there a very bitter juice, but in sucking it, they convert it into honey. (IN I 2)

What does it matter whether God speaks to us amid thorns or amid flowers? (LW VI 13)

How long must we be like adolescents who like candy and cakes better than real nourishing food? (S III 9)

It is far better to eat bread without sugar than sugar without bread. (S XV 1)

Of all the efforts of perfect love, that which is made by acquiescence of spirit in spiritual dryness is the purest and noblest. (T IX 3)

The love that desires to walk to God's will through consolations walks ever in fear of taking the wrong path; but the love that strikes straight through dryness toward the will of God walks in assurance. (T IX 2)

God's shadow is more healthful than His sun. (LR II 21)

I do not say that we may not entertain wishes for deliverance from spiritual dryness, but I do say that we must not set our hearts upon it. (IN IV 4)

God only abases us to lift us up. (LR II 7)

When all fails us, when our spiritual pains have come to their extremity, this word, this disposition—*O Father, into Thy hands I commit my spirit*—can never fail us. (T IX 12)

Do you think our Lady was less the Mother of our Lord when, overwhelmed with affliction, she breathed out that word, *Yes, my Son, because so it has pleased Thee*—than when with exalted voice she sang her *Magnificat*? (LR III 23)

You must choose: is it better that there should be thorns in your garden in order to have roses, or that there should be no roses in order to have no thorns? (LR III 15)

Perseverance

Do not leave out your prayer unless for causes which it is impossible to control. (LR IV 16)

There is nothing which so purges our understanding of its

ignorance and our will of its depraved inclinations as prayer. (IN II 1)

We have never done; we must always begin again and again with a good heart. (LR II 16)

All your happiness depends on perseverance. (C XX)

That mortal who does not desire to love the divine Goodness more loves Him not enough; sufficiency in this divine exercise is not sufficient. (T VI 13)

Perseverance is the most desirable gift we can hope for in this life. (T III 4)

Though perseverance does not come from our power, yet it comes within our power. (T III 4)

To remain at a standstill is impossible; he that gains not, loses; he that ascends not, descends. (T III 1)

Do you not know that you are upon the way, and the way is not made to sit down but to go in? (T III 1)

If one does not ascend the ladder he must descend; if one does not conquer he will be conquered. (S 1 7)

Let us a thousand times a day turn our eyes upon this loving will of God and make ours melt into it. (T VIII 4)

All our childishness proceeds from no fault but this, that we forget that every day we should consider we begin our course of perfection. (LR II 16)

Throughout the day say plenty of ejaculatory prayers, and especially those of the hours when they strike. (LW III 11)

We dare not assure ourselves when we have done a good action that we have done it perfectly. (C VIII)

The three best and most assured marks of lawful inspirations are perseverance, against inconstancy and levity; peace and gentleness of heart, against disquietude and solicitude; humble obedience, against obstinancy and extravagance. (T VIII 13)

Our little fits of anger, of sadness, these little shiverings of the heart, are remains of our maladies, which the sovereign Physician leaves in us in order that we may fear to relapse. (LR VI 9)

He greatly deceives himself who thinks that prayer perfects one without perseverance and obedience. (LR III 44)

Hear Mass in your heart when you cannot hear it elsewhere. (LR VI 28)

Enlarge your heart by a frequent protestation that you will never give in. (LR VI 11)

Holy love may be lost in a moment. (T IV 4)

IV

Living with Our Neighbor

Make many withdrawals into the midst of your heart, whilst you are outwardly in the midst of intercourse and business. (IN II 12)

We must be able to find pleasure in ourselves when alone, and in our neighbor when in his company. (S XXII 5)

On Conduct

To seek the society of others and to shun it are two blame-worthy extremes in the devotion of those who live in the world. (IN III 24)

Do as little children do, who with one hand cling to their father, and with the other gather blackberries along the hedges. (IN III 10)

I recommend to you the gentle and sincere courtesy which offends no one and obliges all, which seeks love rather than honor. (LW IV 2)

Be quite clean and neat, but not particular and dainty. (LW VI 14)

How much easier it is to adjust oneself to others than to bend them to our opinions and wishes. (S II 11)

It is a defect to be so rigorous, boorish and unsociable as not to be willing to take any recreation oneself, or permit others to do so. (IN III 31)

If you have no need of recreation for yourself, you must help to make recreation for those who do need it. (C XIII)

Take care not to let yourself be moody and out of place with those about you. (LR I 4)

We must, if possible, avoid making our devotion troublesome to others. (LW II 6)

That playing and dancing may be permissible, we should take part in such things for the sake of recreation and not merely from fondness of them. (IN III 34)

Make yourself a seller when you are buying, and a buyer when you are selling, and then you will sell and buy justly. (IN III 36)

Though it is lawful to play games, to dance, to adorn oneself, to be present at proper plays, and to feast, yet to have an affection to such things is contrary to devotion, and extremely hurtful and dangerous. (IN I 23)

If anyone helps you more than he is helped by you, realize that you are not his father but only his equal. (s XXII 8)

He that possesses something justly has more right to keep it justly than we have to wish to have it justly. (IN III 14)

Be sure to avoid retaining anything belonging to someone else as far as possible. (LW III 11)

To go to law and not be out of one's mind is scarcely granted to the saints. (LR IV 5)

On Reputation

Trouble not yourself about human judgments. (LW IV 1)

A harvest of virtues should be reaped from a crop of insults and injuries. (s XIV 8)

Too often do we call the truths which offend us by the name of slander. (s VIII 10)

If you wish nothing to cross your life, desire not the reputation or the glory of the world. (LW IV 1)

So long as God is served, what does it matter whether it be by the exaltation or by the defamation of our good reputation? (s VIII 8)

Reputation is but a signboard to show where virtue lodges. (IN III 7)

Excessive fear of losing a good name indicates a great distrust of its foundation, which is the truth of a good life. (IN III 7)

What need for it to be known that you are of good family according to the world, if you are of the household of God? (LW I 10)

When thoughts as to whether people like you or not come into your mind, do not even look at them, for they will always like you as much as God wills. (LR V 5)

Let God do with our life and our reputation and our honor, as He chooses, for it is all His. (LR III 10)

You should not show greater courage than in despising insults. (LW I 12)

Complain as little as possible of the wrongs which are done to you, for it is certain that ordinarily he who complains sins. (IN III 3)

On Speaking

Mere silence is not wisdom, for wisdom consists in

knowing when and how to speak and when and where to keep silent. (s xx 2)

Let your speech be gentle, frank, sincere, straightforward, candid and faithful. (IN III 30)

It is no virtue to be silent by nature, though it is a virtue to bridle one's tongue by reason. (T XI 7)

There is no way of bad speaking other than too much speaking. (LW IV 3)

If charity does not draw us to speak of ourselves and of what belongs to us, we ought to keep silent on the subject. (LR V 2)

Speak little or not at all of oneself or of what belongs to self. (LR II 16)

He who talks little of himself does extremely well, for whether we speak of self in excusing ourselves or in accusing ourselves, whether in praising or in dispraising ourselves, we shall see that our words serve ever as a bait to vanity. (LR V 2)

We often show more disdain by the expression of our mind than the expression of our face. (LW I 3)

If we say less than we should it is easy to add, but having said too much it is hard to take it off. (LW IV 3)

Be brief when you cannot be good. (LR IV 33)

Take it as a certain sign that your charity is not genuine if your words, no matter how true, are not charitable. (S II 12)

It is a sovereign remedy against lying to unsay the lie on the spot. (IN III 8)

One kind word wins more willing service than a hundred harsh orders or stern reproofs. (S VII 9)

Anger is quieted by a gentle word just as fire is quenched by water. (S II 13)

In order that you may always give good news, entertain others as if you came from the other world, for if you talk to them in the language of the parts where they live, it will be no great news to them. (LR IV 35)

Be at peace regarding what is said or done in conversations: for if good, you have something to praise God for, and if bad, something in which to serve God by turning your heart away from it. (LW II 11)

V

The Great Virtues

Forget all that is not of God, and for God, and remain entirely at peace under the guidance of God; this is the height of virtue. (LR V 2)

Among the virtues we should prefer that which is most conformable to our duty, and not that which is most conformable to our inclination. (IN III 1)

True virtue has no limits. (T III 1)

Never do our virtues come to their full stature and measure, till such time as they beget in us desire of progress. (T VIII 8)

As for virtues, we may, of course, ask for them, and in asking for the love of God, we comprise all, for it contains them all. (C XXI)

Resignation

Blessed are they who do not their own will on earth, for God will do it in heaven above. (LR III 17)

Each one ought to cast all his care in God, who indeed sustains the whole world. (LR I 1)

The infant which is within its mother's arms needs only to let her act and to fasten itself to her neck. (LR V 2)

O little cross! thou art dear to me, because neither sense nor nature loves thee, but higher reason alone. (LR IV 33)

Never are we reduced to such an extremity, that we cannot pour forth before the divine Majesty a holy resignation to His most holy will. (C II)

Regard the providence of God in the contradictions which are offered to you, for God permits them in order to detach you from all things and to unite you to Himself. (LR V 5)

Whosoever takes pleasure in God desires faithfully to please God, and in order to please Him, desires to resign himself to Him. (T VIII 1)

Whosoever is not attached to his inclinations, is not impatient when they are contradicted. (LW III 11)

I would have lost my liberty had I not lost my liberty. (LR III 31)

Often it is required to leave God for God, renouncing His

sweetness to serve Him in His sorrows and travails. (LR II 23)

The child readily kisses his mother when she gives him sugar; but it is a sign that he loves her greatly if he kisses her after she has given him wormwood. (IN IV 14)

There is no clearer proof of affection for a thing than distress at the loss thereof. (IN III 14)

We must never so form our opinions as not to be ready, if necessary, willingly to give them up. (C XIV)

When we abandon everything, our Lord takes care of everything and orders everything. (C II)

When will it be that, dead before God, we shall live again to this new life in which we shall no more will to do anything, but shall let God will all that we have to do? (LR II 4)

Devotion

Devotion is no other thing than a spiritual nimbleness and vivacity by which charity works in us, or we in her, readily and heartily. (IN I 1)

Charity and devotion differ no more, the one from the other, than the flame from the fire. (IN I 1)

The true essence of devout love consists in the movement and effusion of the heart which immediately follows complacency and ends in union. (T I 7)

He who desires love ardently shall shortly love with ardor. (T XII 2)

If charity be a milk, devotion is its cream; if it be a plant, devotion is its flower. (IN I 3)

Man gives himself wholly by love, and gives himself as much as he loves. (T X 3)

Such as love is, such is the zeal which is its ardor. (T X 12)

We must bring the razor to the division of the self and the spirit. (LR II 16)

To live according to the spirit is to think, speak and act according to the virtues that are in the spirit, and not according to the sense and sentiments which are in the flesh. (LR III 47)

Feeling and sweetness in devotion may come from the friend or the enemy. (LR I 2)

The less we live after our own tastes, and the less of choice there is in our actions, the more of solidity there is in our devotion. (LW II 6)

True devotion does no harm whatever, but rather gives perfection to all things; but when it goes contrary to our lawful vocation, then without doubt it is false. (IN I 3)

True devotion advances boldly, without stopping to worry about details. (S XX 9)

Complacency draws the divine sweetness into our heart; but the love of benevolence makes our heart pass out of itself. (T V 9)

How happy we shall be if one day we change our own self into that love, which, making us no more separate, will perfectly empty us of all multiplicity! (LR II 16)

Generous devotion does not wish to have companions in all that it does, but only in its aim, which is the glory of God and the advancement of our neighbor in divine love. (C I)

Holy Indifference

Ask for nothing and refuse nothing. (LR III 50)

The indifferent heart is as a ball of wax in the hands of its God, receiving with equal readiness all the impressions of the divine pleasure. (T IX 4)

Remain in indifference as to having or not having spiritual goods. (LR V 5)

Holy indifference goes beyond resignation: for it loves nothing except for the love of God's will. (T IX 4)

If I desire pure water only, what care I whether it be served in a golden vessel or in a glass. (T IX 4)

We must not only consent for God to strike us, but we must let it be in the place which He pleases. (LW VII 9)

You are quite willing to have a cross, but you want to have the choice. (LW VI 2)

The truly indifferent soul would prize hell more with God's will than heaven without it. (T IX 4)

Where there is true indifference there can be no trouble or sadness. (C VIII)

Young apprentices in the love of God gird themselves, choose mortifications as seems good to themselves and try to do their own will at the same time as that of God; but old masters of the craft let themselves be girded by others and go by ways which according to their own inclination they do not choose. (LR VI 24)

What should it matter to us whether it is by the deserts or by the meadows we go, if God is with us and we go into Paradise? (LR VI 3)

She is an all-pure soul who cannot love the Paradise of God, but only the God of Paradise. (T X 5)

You must remain calm and indifferent between desolation and consolation. (C II)

To leave off doing a good when God pleases, and to return from half way when God's will ordains it—these are marks of a most perfect indifference. (T IX 6)

We are to omit nothing which is requisite to bring the work which God has put into our hands to a happy issue, yet upon the condition that, if the event be contrary, we should lovingly embrace it. (T IX 6)

Most injuries are more happily met by the indifference which is shown for them than by any other means. (LW I 11)

It is a greater virtue to eat without choice what is set before you, than always to choose the worst. (IN III 23)

O God! How this word *acceptance* is great with love! (T IX 2)

Never make a difficulty as to receiving what God sends you on the left. (LR I 2)

To the detached soul it is all one to her whether she serve

God by meditating, or serve Him by bearing with her neighbor-both are the will of God, but the bearing with her neighbor is necessary at that time. (LW III 11)

The holy indifferent soul which wills nothing, but lets God will what pleases Him, should be said to have its will in a simple and general state of waiting. (T IX 15)

What matters it to a truly loving soul whether God be served by this means or by another? (LR III 25)